WHY SETTLE FOR A SLICE, WHEN YOU CAN HAVE THE WHOLE PIE!

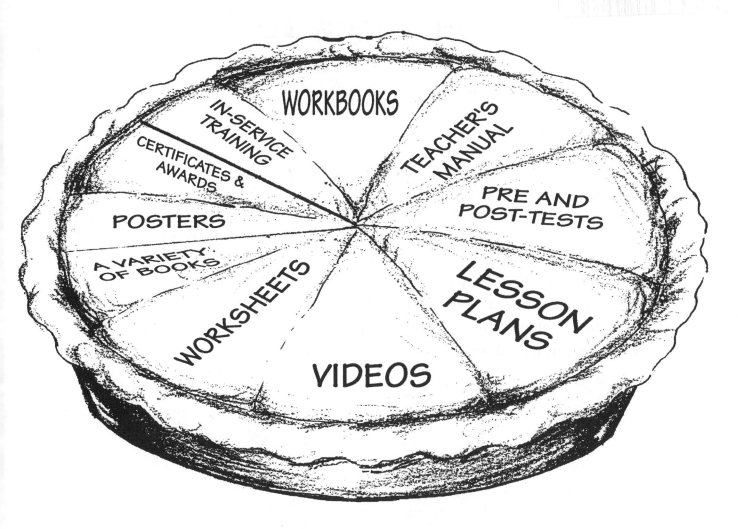

The workbooks are designed for K-12 and are a very important component of SETCLAE's comprehensive, Africentric, multicultural curriculum.

SETCLAE
Self-Esteem Through Culture Leads to Academic Excellence

7th Grade Workbook

Harambee Session Illustrations by Reginald Mackey
First edition, first printing
Copyright 1992 by Doriel R. Mackay, M.A. and Jawanza Kunjufu, Ph.D.

(Kiswahili for Dependable & Cheerful)

African American Images
Chicago, Illinois

ACKNOWLEDGMENTS

I would like to thank the following individuals for their contributions in making this workbook possible:

*Dr. Jawanza Kunjufu and Folami Prescott,
for their vision in creating this model curriculum for our youth.*

*Ms. Rita Smith-Kunjufu,
for her clear directions and serenity.*

*Dr. Gwendolyn Brooks,
my distinguished Professor of English at Chicago State University,
for holding the torch high and lighting my way.*

*Haki Madhubuti,
my esteemed Professor of English at Chicago State University,
for being an excellent teacher.*

*Dr. Margaret Duggar,
Professor of English at Chicago State University
for sharing her knowledge and humor during my studies.*

*Ms. Kimberly Vann,
African American Images, for her coordinating efforts and patience.*

*Ms. Adrian Payton-Williams,
African American Images, for her technical support.*

*Ms. Charlene Snelling,
Resource Librarian, Chicago State University for her
encouragement and finally, the Creator of the Universe
without whom nothing would exist.*

Doriel R. Mackay, M.A.

The SETCLAE Workbook
Seventh Grade
TABLE OF CONTENTS

INTRODUCTION

Jambo mwanafunzi (Hello students)! Welcome to SETCLAE! This program was designed to help you achieve excellence in your studies in school by making you aware of:

Your history
Goals to strive toward
Helping you to achieve self-esteem
Developing love for your family, friends,
classmates and communities

It is our hope, we teachers (mwalimu), that as we try to impart this knowledge to you and share some basic principles with each other that we both shall grow. These principles are:

Umoja - Unity
Ujima - Collective work and responsibility
Ujamaa - Cooperative Economics
Nia - Purpose
Kuumba - Creativity
Imani - Faith
Kujichagulia - Self-determination

So, HARAMBEE (Let's pull together) for together we shall win!

How to Make the Most of Your SETCLAE Journey

In order to get the full benefit from this workbook, you will need to study some additional books as well participate in some activities and exercises.

Here are a few suggestions that will help you master this material:

1. Look over the vocabulary list of Kiswahili words. Kiswahili is the language chosen by the Pan-African Congress in 1974 to be an international language amongst peoples of African origin all around the world.
2. Use a variety of materials for your art work such as: markers, pencils, crayons, paint.
3. Look at magazines like *Ebony, Essence, Jet, YSB, The Source, Emerge, African Commentary, Black Enterprise* and any other material that discusses African and African American people. They are filled with relevant information, lessons from history, and illustrations of Black life.
4. Use your ideas to create poems, raps, skits, songs, dances, dramatic presentations, speeches, plays, books, articles, and letters to share your insight with others.
5. Take your Journal entries seriously. They may be the raw materials for your best-selling autobiography.
6. Use the illustrations of each Harambee Time for bulletin boards, posters and other visual displays.
7. When working in Harambee Groups, encourage members to take on tasks according to talents and interests. Each group should identify someone to fulfill the following roles:

Moderator	Illustrator
Timekeeper	Rapper/Poet
Reporter	Observer
Recorder	

Of course, one person can perform several of these roles simultaneously.

8. Let your Kuumba (creativity) flow as you create your own poetry, dramatic presentations, and speeches.
9. Share your newfound knowledge with your family and friends.
10. Always remember: everyone is a "mwalimu mwanafunzi" (teacher and student).
11. Never forget what SETCLAE stands for: Self-Esteem Through Culture Leads to Academic Excellence!!!

Now, let's put on our critical thinking caps and begin. The first thing we would like to do is what is known as a profile. A profile helps you to see clearly how you feel about yourself and others by asking questions. Then as you study the books and go through the activities, you will begin to discover a new way to think about yourself, a better way of feeling and another way to look at the world around you.

Correlation of SETCLAE Lessons to Academic Objectives

In an effort to accommodate the implementation of SETCLAE into the existing curriculum in your school, the Harambee Time sessions have been correlated to the most common academic objectives for this grade level. *The Typical Course of Study* for kindergarten through twelfth grade was compiled by World Book Educational Products. Curriculum materials such as the Nault-Caswell-Brain Analysis of Courses of Study and others from The National Council of Teachers of Mathematics, English, and Social Studies were analyzed in the preparation of the study guide.

Please use this guide to help give SETCLAE a home in your setting. You will soon see that the program is a welcome and valuable member of the family the Harambee Time can be effective in "pulling us together" as we build Tomorrow's Leaders. We also encourage you to incorporate the learning and classroom management styles (e.g. student-made materials and Harambee groups respectively) used in SETCLAE into all subjects taught. And share your success stories with your colleagues!

SS - Social Studies   LA - Language Arts   HT - Health   MT - Mathematics

1 -- Let Me Introduce Myself
- LA Note taking skills
- Report writing skills

2 -- Bonding
- LA Note taking skills
- Research skills
- Listening and speech activities
- Collective decision making

3 -- Rules, Rights, and Responsibilities
- LA Deductive Reasoning

4 -- Positive People Praising
- LA Use of periodicals
- Listening/spelling

5 -- Goal Setting
- SS Our American Culture
- U.S. Political System
- African American History

6 --- I Can Be!
- Career Education
- LA Using basic reference materials

7 --- Me and My Family
- SS U.S. Geography
- Our American culture
- Our Native background

8 --- Names We Call Ourselves
- LA Dictionary work
- Extended vocabulary
- Our American culture

9 --- The Color Question
- LA Advanced dictionary work
- Extended vocabulary
- Listening and speech

10 --- *Lessons* Video with Dr. Jawanza Kunjufu
- LA Critique
- SS Our American culture
- HT Type and functions of food
- Body's utilization of food

SETCLAE Vocabulary Means WORD POWER!!!

There is a great deal of power in having a large vocabulary. With a greater understanding of more words, there comes a greater understanding of the world around us and an ability to express what we see, think, and attempt to comprehend. Use the words listed below that are introduced in the Harambee Times noted. Use them in your home, school, among friends and others. Just watch for the power!!!

Harambee Time #3
impression
violate

Harambee Time #4
skit
dramatize

Harambee Time #6
automation
unusual

Harambee Time #8
diaspora

Harambee Time #9
oppression

Harambee Time #11
civilization
continent

Harambee Time #12
exhibit
sphinx

Harambee Time #14
rebellion

Harambee Time #15
constitution

Harambee Time #18
distinctive

Harambee Time #19
dialect
appropriate

Harambee Time #27
significant

Harambee Time #28
verdict
exemplify

Harambee Time #31
economics

Harambee Time #32
exemplary
entail
puberty
transition

The SETCLAE Student Profile

Instructions

Please answer the following questions on the answer sheet and think very hard about how you feel before answering each one. THERE ARE NO RIGHT OR WRONG ANSWERS. WE WANT YOUR ANSWERS.

Part I

Read each statement or question. If it is true for you, circle the letter "a". If it is not true for you, circle "b". Answer every question, even if it's hard to decide. (Just think about yourself and what's important to you.) Select only one answer for each question.

1. I like to be alone sometimes.	a. Yes	b. No
2. I enjoy public speaking.	a. Yes	b. No
3. Cleaning up should be done collectively.	a. Yes	b. No
4. School will help me to accomplish my own goals.	a. Yes	b. No
5. I enjoy looking for positive things to say about people.	a. Yes	b. No
6. I have personal goals.	a. Yes	b. No
7. I would rather do an extra credit project by myself than with a small group.	a. Yes	b. No
8. I get upset when things don't go my way.	a. Yes	b. No
9. School is boring most of the time.	a. Yes	b. No
10. I speak more than one dialect.	a. Yes	b. No
11. If I don't see a trash can, I throw my trash on the ground.	a. Yes	b. No
12. I like participating in special projects like science fairs and spelling bees.	a. Yes	b. No
13. When the truth is hard to say, I don't say it.	a. Yes	b. No
14. My friends are more important to me than my family.	a. Yes	b. No
15. My neighborhood is a good place to live in.	a. Yes	b. No

16. I can get any job I want, if I work at it hard enough.   a. Yes   b. No

17. I like being with people that are different from me.   a. Yes   b. No

18. I like me!   a. Yes   b. No

19. Do you believe you can have your own
    business when you get older?   a. Yes   b. No

20. The contribution I make to the world is not as
    important as the contributions of more famous people.   a. Yes   b. No

21. African Americans have not made many achievements
    in math, science, technology, and business.   a. Yes   b. No

22. If I could, I would make friends with people of all races.   a. Yes   b. No

23. Black people are not able to compete with
    others in many areas.   a. Yes   b. No

24. I want to be able to speak Standard
    English in certain situations.   a. Yes   b. No

Part II

Read each item carefully. If it is something that is important to you, select "a". If it is not important to you (it doesn't really matter or has nothing to do with you), select "b". Take your time and think about it. THERE ARE NO RIGHT OR WRONG ANSWERS. WE WANT TO KNOW YOUR FEELINGS.

1. Helping others   a. Important to me   b. Not important to me

2. What others think of me   a. Important to me   b. Not important to me

3. Reading in a study group   a. Important to me   b. Not important to me

4. Television as a way to receive
   most of my information   a. Important to me   b. Not important to me

5. Solving problems by fighting   a. Important to me   b. Not important to me

6. Learning about my family
   members - dead and living   a. Important to me   b. Not important to me

7. Working with others on short and
   long-term projects   a. Important to me   b. Not important to me

8. Doing whatever my friends do   a. Important to me   b. Not important to me

9. Wearing expensive clothes   a. Important to me   b. Not important to me

10. Doing well in school   a. Important to me   b. Not important to me

11. Speaking up for myself and
    my ideas   a. Important to me   b. Not important to me

12. Being positive most of the time   a. Important to me   b. Not important to me

13. Living conditions in Africa   a. Important to me   b. Not important to me

Part III

Read each statement carefully. Read the choices and select "a" if the statement accurately describes you and your feelings. Select "b" if the statement does not accurately describe you and your feelings.

If asked to describe my personality to someone I'd never met, I would use statements like:

1. a leader   a. Yes   b. No

2. confident   a. Yes   b. No

3. mature   a. Yes   b. No

4. critical of others   a. Yes   b. No

5. proud of my culture   a. Yes   b. No

6. easily bored   a. Yes   b. No

7. Africa is a dark continent filled with hunger,
   poverty and ignorance.   a. True   b. False

8. I can list five living African American men that are doing positive things in their family, business, church, community, or some other organization.
   List them below.

1) _____
2) _____
3) _____
4) _____
5) _____

9. Select the one that is most important to you. Choose only one!
          a. being popular   b. doing well in school

Part IV

Read the following statements and choices for answers carefully. Then pick the answer that most accurately describes your feelings. Circle the letter in front of your answer.

THERE ARE NO RIGHT OR WRONG ANSWERS. Choose the answer that is right for YOU.

1. When my friends have fun without me, I
   a. am happy that they are having fun.
   b. don't even think about it.
   c. wish they weren't having fun without me.

2. When I hear something negative about a person, I
   a. can't wait to tell someone else.
   b. talk to the person to see how I can help.
   c. try to find out more, because it's interesting.

3. When someone says something about me that is not good but is true, I
   a. get upset.
   b. don't want to be around them anymore.
   c. listen and learn from their observations.

4. When someone makes fun of me,
   a. I get upset.   c. I laugh with them.
   b. I am hurt.   d. I make a joke of it.
   e. I don't like it.

5. When I am talking to someone, most of the time I look
   a. at their hands.   c. at the floor.
   d. into their eyes.   d. all around.

6. I always make sure I am neat and clean in my appearance:
   a. never
   b. once in a while
   c. most of the time

7. Money is important for:
   a. buying expensive clothes   c. buying whatever I want
   b. building the community in which we live   d. saving for future plans

8. A girl becomes a woman when (select the answer that is most important to you),
   a. she has a baby.
   b. her body becomes more developed (she has breasts and hair under her arms).
   c. she takes care of herself and her family.
   d. she can talk back to her mother.
   e. she has a boyfriend.

9. When I do poorly on my schoolwork, I
   a. don't really care.
   b. know I tried my best.
   c. know I should try harder.
   d. know it's only because I can't do any better.
   e. know the teacher gave us work that was too hard or boring.

10. In my involvement with organizations, I
    a. like to hold a leadership position.
    b. like to work as a team.
    c. don't like doing the dirty work.
    d. often disagree with other members.

11. When I need help, I
    a. get frustrated.
    b. ask for it.
    c. try to figure it out myself.

12. I pick my friends because
    a. they look good.
    b. they are cool.
    c. they are understanding.
    d. they have something to offer me.

13. I am glad I am the race I am.
    a. Yes   b. No

14. I chose the answer above because
    a. I am proud of my heritage.
    b. I should be glad.
    c. I study my history and culture.
    d. my friends say it's important.

15. I like my favorite music because
    a. of its rhythm for dancing.
    b. of its positive messages.
    c. of its ability to help me relax.
    d. the rappers curse and insult women.
    e. the videos are nice.

16. A boy becomes a man when
    a. he can handle drugs and crime.
    b. he makes a baby.
    c. he takes responsibility for his actions.
    d. he can fight well.

17. When I attend assemblies or special events, I like to sit
    a. in the middle of the auditorium.
    b. in the front of the auditorium.
    c. in the back of the auditorium.

18. When I set a goal, I
    a. expect someone to make it happen for me.
    b. plan how I will do it and make the first step.
    c. just think about it very hard.
    d. ask my friends to get me started.

19. When the teacher leaves the room, I
    a. talk.
    b. stop doing my work.
    c. look at who is being disobedient.
    d. find something quiet to do once I finish my work.

20. Learning about one's culture and heritage is very important and helps me feel good about who I am.
    a. Yes
    b. No

21. I like my favorite television program because
    a. it's very funny.
    b. I enjoy the action.
    c. I enjoy the "scenery" (cars, clothes, houses, etc.).
    d. it is educational.
    e. it makes me think and discuss important issues with others.

22. I am beautiful because I have
    a. light skin.
    b. dark skin.
    c. natural hair.
    d. long hair.
    e. a thin shape.

23. Answering these questions was
    a. very enjoyable.
    b. no big deal.
    c. a good way to take a closer look at my personal development.

24. Africa has many cities.
    a. True   b. False

25. Africa is the Motherland of Black people all over the world.
    a. True   b. False

26. Egypt, also known as Kemet (which means Land of the Blacks) is in Africa, which is the cradle of civilization.
   a. True   b. False

27. African people have always resisted domination all over the world.
   a. True   b. False

28. Africa is mostly jungle.
   a. True   b. False

29. Tarzan movies show you what Africa is like and used to be like.
   a. True   b. False

30. Africa is a continent on which there is a cultural unity more important than the differences we hear about in the news.
   a. True   b. False

Using the definitions on the right, place the letter that you feel best describes each of the seven principles listed (Nguzo Saba).

____ 31. UMOJA

____ 32. KUJICHAGULIA

____ 33. UJIMA

____ 34. UJAMAA

____ 35. NIA

____ 36. KUUMBA

____ 37. IMANI

a. to build our stores and businesses and profit from them together

b. to have a collective goal of building and developing our community

c. to always be creative in the ways we improve our communities

d. being determined to speak up for ourselves

e. to work on challenges together and feel responsible as a group

f. to believe in ourselves that we will do great things

g. to keep in touch with and offer support to friends, neighbors, and community

Let Me Introduce Myself

Materials:
- Pen
- Index Cards
- Chairs (arranged in a circle)

Using an index card, tell us:

- Your full name and birthplace
- Number of siblings
- Your favorite movie/TV show/commercial
- How far you plan to go in school
- A career that interests you
- Something you do well
- A person you admire
- A person you would like to meet
- A positive word to describe you that begins with the same letter as your first name (e.g., Excellent Edward, Dynamic Denise, Cheerful Charles)

Journal:
Write down how you feel about having to stand in front of others and introduce yourself. Were you comfortable? Were you pleased with yourself?

Procedure:

Habari Gani - What is the news? Let's see how well you can present yourself to others supplying the most basic information about yourself.

Postscript:
Share with the other students their introductions and nice qualities you see they have neglected to mention.

Materials: (HG)

- Completed I.D. Cards
- Personal Photos for I.D. Cards
- Glue or Stapler
- 5 sticks to attach to each group's flag

NOTES:

_____
_____
_____
_____
_____
_____
_____
_____
_____
_____
_____
_____
_____
_____
_____
_____

Journal:

In your journal, write about other ways in which you would like to bond with your friends and family members. What specifically would you like to do?

Bonding

Harambee Time #2

Procedure:

Look at the number on your card. That is the number of your Harambee Group. Sit in the area designated for your group and exchange information with your classmates.

Choose a name for your group from the list below:
- #1   Umoja, Kujichagulia, Ujima, Ujamaa, Nia, Kuumba, Imani
- #2   Nigeria, Kenya, Egypt, Azania, Tanzania
- #3   Ashanti, Chagga, Pondo, Fanti, Ikoma
- #4   Morehouse, Hampton U., Spelman, Tuskegee U., Howard U.
- #5   Scientists, Lawyers, Artists, Educators, Farmers

For more informations about groups, #2, #3 and #4, read "Something You Should Know."

Bonding is an activity that can take place in your home, your school or at work. Bonding means that people work together and care for one another. Try to picture situations in which you are bonding with other people. Jot these situations in your Notes section.

Postscript:

Working with your Harambee Group, discuss the meaning of shared activities.

Rules, Rights, and Responsibilities

List some of the basic rights that every human being has.

_____
_____
_____
_____
_____
_____
_____
_____
_____
_____
_____
_____
_____
_____
_____
_____
_____
_____

Procedure:

Discuss these questions with your Harambee Group, then share their responses with the class.

What kind of people assign rules, rights and responsibilities?

_____

What types of rules and responsibilities are given to you?

_____

What do you think your rights are as a child?

_____

What do you think your rights are as a student?

_____

What are your responsibilities to your teacher?

_____

Do you have any responsibilities to your classmates?

_____

What responsibilities do you have at home?

_____

Journal:

List your impressions of what it will be like to be an adult with lots of responsibilities.

Postscript:

Discuss with your classmates events in which peoples' rights were violated. Analyze how slavery violated certain rights.

Materials:

- Coloring Materials
- Paper
- Pen
- *Great Negroes*

NOTES:

_____

_____

_____

_____

_____

_____

_____

_____

_____

_____

_____

_____

_____

_____

_____

_____

_____

_____

_____

Journal:

Write a thank you letter to someone who makes you feel good about yourself.

Positive People Praising

Procedure:

There are two ways you can treat others: tear someone down through gossip, or encourage them with kind words. People that do not feel good about themselves gossip and find it difficult to praise others. People that feel good about themselves praise others because they know they're also good. Write one characteristic, positive trait or idea about each student on a sheet of notebook paper.

Become a Positive People Praising person! List some ways you can help someone feel better about him or herself.

1. _____
2. _____
3. _____
4. _____
5. _____

From *Great Negroes* draw a picture of someone you most admire and write three paragraphs about what he or she did that was special.

Postscript:

Discuss some other great people that you know about. Look through *Great Negroes* and talk about their achievements. Was it always easy for them to succeed or did they have to struggle?

Do a skit about a famous person dramatizing some important event in his or her life.

Materials:
✏ Pen
✏ Abdul and the
Designer Tennis
Shoes

Place these sentences in correct sequence to see how easy it is to set and accomplish a goal.

1. He goes to the library.   _____
2. Michael types the essay.   _____
3. Michael decides to write about Egypt.   _____
4. He gives his assignment to the teacher.   _____
5. He writes about what he has read.   _____
6. Michael reads books and articles about Egypt.   _____

Procedure:
What is the importance of goals?

What are long-term goals?

What are short-term goals?

Are wishes and dreams a part of how to develop goals?

List some of the most important things that you would like to have or do in the next six months. Next to these things try to think of three things that you will have to do in order to accomplish your goals. Remember to tell yourself frequently, I want to... so I will...

Goal: _____   Goal: _____
1)_____   1) _____
2) _____   2) _____
3) _____   3) _____

Goal: _____   Goal: _____
1) _____   1) _____
2) _____   2) _____
3) _____   3) _____

Journal:
Write down how much easier it is to accomplish your goals if you stay focused. Think about some of your short-term and long-term goals. Write down some of the things you would have to do to achieve them.

Postscript:
Discuss Abdul's greatest dream. How was he keeping himself from realizing his dream? Is it really important to have faith in your talents? Should you practice if you want to be really good at something? Share some of your hobbies with a friend or classmate and explain how they might be related to accomplishing a goal you may have set for yourself.

Materials:

✏ Help Wanted
Section from a
Major Newspaper

✏ Lessons From
History, Chapter 5

NOTES:

_____
_____
_____
_____
_____
_____
_____
_____
_____
_____
_____
_____
_____
_____
_____
_____
_____
_____
_____

Journal:
How important is it to
enjoy your career?

I Can Be!

Harambee
Time
#6

Procedure:

Some careers involve manual labor, while others require strictly mental skills. Referring to the Help Wanted section of the newspaper, answer the following questions:

1. Which occupations require a college degree?
2. Which careers require a great deal of public contact?
3. Which careers would allow you to travel extensively?
4. Which careers demand manual labor?
5. Which occupations have a high income potential?
6. Name three types of careers which are considered physically dangerous?
7. What are some jobs that may exist in Africa that do not exist in America?

List some of your skills that will help you have a successful career?
What career are you interested in pursuing?
Would you enjoy it?

Postscript:

In *Lessons*, Chapter 5 there are some important people discussed. Why are their achievements singled out? Are there people today whose accomplishments are unusual? See if you can name three people.

Materials:
- Choosing a Path
- A Dictionary
- Pen
- Construction Paper
- Markers

NOTES:
_____

_____

_____

_____

_____

_____

Journal:
A family is more than mother, father, sister, and brother. It includes aunts, uncles, cousins and grandparents. This is called an extended family. Write the names of members of your extended family and what you like most about them.

Postscript:
Read *Choosing a Path*. Try to understand how the families in this story affected the behavior of the two sons. Can your family help you do better? Can your family contribute to destructive behavior also?

Procedure:
What does the word family mean to you?

How is family defined in the dictionary?

Describe your family (how many people are in it, the person you spend the most time with, how you help each other?)

What is the difference between family and friends?

Is family important? If so, why? Why do family members get on your nerves so much?

What kind of activities does your family do together? What would you like to do together?

Get long pieces of construction paper and draw pictures of your family engaged in various activities. Suggested pictures are:
your family picnic or barbecue, birthday party, graduation, etc.

Names We Call Ourselves

Materials:
- ✏ *Lessons*, p. 86, 87, 93-5 (poem)
- ✏ *Shining Legacy*, p. 32-38 (The Saga of Malcolm X)

NOTES:

_____
_____
_____
_____
_____
_____
_____
_____
_____
_____
_____
_____
_____

Procedure:
Read the poem by Margaret Burroughs.

Do you like all the names that she uses to describe people? Why or why not? What names can you think of to describe your race? Can you identify some African Americans who have changed their names to African names? In *Shining Legacy*, what famous leader changed his name? What are some of the reasons most African Americans do not have African names?

Our names can tell us where our roots are which help us to shape our identity and appreciate our culture. It's that unique history that gives people their roots.

Journal:
Give yourself and your family a name that means something to you in terms of your African heritage. Write down the meaning of your special name.

Postscript:
Discuss the meaning of the diaspora and how we lost our family names. Can we ever find out who our families were in Africa and what those family names were?

Materials:
✏ Your Critical
  Thinking Skills

NOTES:

_____
_____
_____
_____
_____
_____
_____
_____
_____
_____
_____
_____
_____
_____
_____
_____

Procedure:
Answer the following questions:

What are some of the problems that people encounter because of their race? Do you ever dislike or mistreat other people simply because of their skin color? How you change this type of attitude? How did the different races come into existence? What are some of these theories? Do people of different races differ in ability? Are they equal? Are they superior or inferior?

Look through magazines and cut out different pictures of Africans and African Americans in all shades. Describe, using at least 5 adjectives, how they appear to you.

```
_____
_____
_____
_____
_____
_____
_____
_____
_____
_____
_____
_____
_____
_____
```

Journal:
Write down how you feel about your color. Be honest. If there is discomfort or uncertainty about this issue, discuss your feelings with your parents or another family member.

Postscript:
In America, African Americans are in the minority, but when you look at the entire world, they are in the majority. What are some of the problems that are faced by African Americans and not by other groups of people here?

Materials:
✏ *Lessons* video
✏ Television and Video Recorder

Procedure:
Watch the *Lessons* video, take notes, and answer these questions: What things are most important to you? Why are they important? In what areas do you perform best? Is it because of natural ability or constant practice? Why is time such an important resource? How do you use it wisely? What's the most important decision you will make? Why is a natural high better than an artificial one? Why is it important to know your history? What lessons have you learned from history? How will they help you avoid making similar mistakes?

Postscripts:
Exercise your right to freedom of speech and write a letter to your neighborhood paper or major metropolitan paper abour something you are dissatisfied about. After all, so many of our ancestors died so that African Americans could have equal rights. Plan a trip to a newspaper office to see the presses, newsroom, and reporters in action.

Journal:
Write about who you think the bravest person in history was and why.

Materials: (HG)
- 🖉 *Lessons*, Chapter 1
- 🖉 Pen
- 🖉 Map
- 🖉 Encyclopedia

NOTES:

_____
_____
_____
_____
_____
_____
_____

Read Chapter 1 in *Lessons*, the Beginning of Civilization. Next, take your map and try to identify all the countries in Africa and the great bodies of water surrounding the continent. Develop a rap, skit, poem, story, or illustration entitled, "The Great African Empires of Mali, Songhay and Ghana."

Journal:
In your journal, describe your impression of Africa and explain why you would like to visit that continent someday.

Africa, The Continent

Procedure:
Form Harambee Groups. Each group should be assigned to do some research on one country in Africa. Some information to include on each country should encompass the following:

pp. 1-2:   Geographical Facts about the Birthplace of Humanity
pp. 3-4:   Science, Education, and Architecture in Ancient Africa
pp. 5-6:   African Kings & Queens/The Truth About the Greeks
pp. 7-8:   Empires and Religion in Africa
pp. 9-10: African Explorers, Resources, and City Life

Postscript:
Discuss the meaningful contributions that Africans have made to culture and civilization in ancient times. Share this information with your family members.

Materials: (HG)
- Bus
- Lunch
- Paper

Procedures:
Traveling with your Harambee Group, take a trip to a museum where there are exhibits from Egypt on display. See if you can locate these artifacts:

A pyramid	sphinx
A ankh	mummy
papyrus	scepter

NOTES:

_____
_____
_____
_____
_____
_____
_____

Journal:
Imagine that you are in Ancient Egypt. What do you see around you? What are the people doing? Write down all of your observations.

Read and discuss the following in small groups:

Many villages in present-day Egypt are built on the site of ancient ones. They lie near the river but on high ground out of reach of the inundation. The mounts on which they sit are made even higher by the fact that centuries of mud-brick rubble have been piled on them. As one house fell down, another was built on top of it. There is therefore little archaeological evidence of the earliest villages, especially as the decaying mud-brick has been used as fertilizer by generations of peasants. Whole villages have been lost this way. Most of the archaeological evidence for village life comes from the remains of villages built to house the families of craftsmen and officials working on the royal tombs. These villages, situated near the tombs, were in remote desert places. When the work force was no longer needed, the sites were abandoned. In time, they fell into ruin, but the sand which covered the ruins has preserved them.
* *The Egyptian World*, Margaret Oliphant, Warwick Press, 1989.

Postscript:
Pretend that you are a great Egyptian ruler, priest, scribe or architect. Talk about some of your duties and responsibilities.

Materials:
- Markers
- Paper
- *Lessons*, Chapter 2
- Dictionary
- Encyclopedia

NOTES:

_____

_____

_____

_____

_____

_____

_____

_____

_____

Procedure:

Using Chapter 2 in *Lessons*, try to get a clear understanding of what the African Triangle means. Then draw a map of the three continents involved, name them and the bodies of water in between.

How were Africans transported to the countries within the African Triangle? _____

Name some of the crops that were produced?_____
_____

List some of the languages that are spoken in the continents of the African Triangle? _____

_____

Do you believe African Americans live in Brazil, Mexico, or Haiti?___

_____

What route was used during the Middle Passage? _____

_____

What cargo was obtained throughout the African Triangle? _____

_____

Postscript:

Discuss some of the great warriors in Chapter 4 in *Lessons*. Were they really brave? Do you agree with their strategies? What, if anything, would you have done differently?

Journal:

Choose a continent in the African Triangle and using an encyclopedia, write a one page report about your selection.

Freedom Fighters

Materials:
📖 *Shining Legacy,* pp. 18-20

Procedure:
Answer the following questions:

How would you define freedom?

Do African Americans and Pan-African people have true freedom?

What are some serious problems that exist in some African countries?

How would you solve them?

NOTES:

_____
_____
_____
_____
_____
_____
_____
_____

Journal:
Imagine that you have to fight for your freedom. Plan your strategy, then write about it.

Postscript:
History has taught us that some people in America tried to help runaway slaves. What was the Underground Railroad? Were the slaves happy? Look at *Shining Legacy* p. 8 about the Amistad ship rebellion. Pretend that you are on the ship and do a mock dialogue of the slaves plotting their attack. Have two teams, one of the slaves and the other of the shipmates.

Materials:
✏ *Shining Legacy,*
   p. 28-29 (Poem)

NOTES:

_____

_____

_____

_____

_____

_____

_____

_____

_____

_____

_____

_____

_____

_____

_____

_____

Procedure:
Read the poem, "The Ballad of Rosa Parks". The incident with Rosa Parks was not the only type of discrimination that African Americans have had to endure. What other forms of discrimination existed before the 1960's? What were the Jim Crow laws? Could African Americans eat in the same restaurants as European restaurants? Why or why not? Who were some of the Freedom Fighters who led the civil rights movement and assisted Rosa Parks?

Journal:
Imagine what it must have been like not to be able to sit in any vacant seat on the bus. Would you have acted as Rosa Parks did or abided by the law? Explain why or why not in your journal.

Postscript:
Are there any laws today that you would like to see changed?
Think about some positive steps you could take to get them changed.

Materials: (HG)
- *Lessons*, Chapter 7
- Poster Boards or Long Sheets of Paper
- Coloring Materials
- Pen

Procedure:

Read Chapter 7 in *Lessons* and answer these questions:

1. What is the lesson you should learn from freedom fighters such as Queen Nzinga, Harriet Tubman, Malcolm X and Martin Luther King, Jr.?

2. How can you stop feeling inferior to other races?

3. How should you define "good" hair?

4. Why is racial unity important?

5. How important is education?

Working with your Harambee Group, choose one of the following ways to illustrate a lesson from history:

Create a skit, write a rap, or draw a mural (using several poster boards or long sheets of paper).

Journal:

Record your impressions of the strengths of African people and how these strengths will help you endure.

Postscript:

Discuss why history is meaningful. Why should we try to remember the past? How can studying the past contribute to planning the future and helping to avoid mistakes? Has the history of African people been kept from African Americans? What effect can it have on people to not know their history?

African American Excellence and Leadership

Materials:
✐ Magazines (Ebony, Jet, Black Enterprise, and Essence)
✐ Great Negroes

Procedure:
Pick three of the careers listed, then look through magazines such as Ebony, Jet, Black Enterprise, and Essence for the names of men and women who are excelling in their areas of interest. Write the names of those individuals beneath the appropriate categories.

Categories:
Business, Medicine, Science/Math, Computers, TV/Radio, Education, Politics, Engineering, Human Rights, and Writing

Journal:
Write down how it would feel to be a prominent leader one day?
Would you be a public speaker?
A scientist?
An engineer?

Write your choices here:

A. _____   A. _____
1. _____   1. _____
2. _____   2. _____
3. _____   3. _____
4. _____   4. _____

B. _____   B. _____
1. _____   1. _____
2. _____   2. _____
3. _____   3. _____
4. _____   4. _____

C. _____   C. _____
1. _____   1. _____
2. _____   2. _____
3. _____   3. _____
4. _____   4. _____

Choose one man and one woman to profile in a report you will share with your class.

_____
MAN

_____
WOMAN

Postscript:
Look through Great Negroes and list the various types of leadership roles that various people played.
How are they different or the same?

Black Culture

Procedure:

Read the assigned pages from *Lessons*, then discuss them with your classmates.

NOTES:

_____

_____

_____

_____

_____

_____

_____

_____

_____

_____

_____

_____

_____

_____

_____

_____

_____

_____

_____

_____

_____

Answer these questions:

What is culture? What are some components of Black culture? How do you demonstrate aspects of Black culture?

Each Harambee Group should choose one of the following categories and create a display or an oral presentation based on that cultural component. Use the page numbers for reference.

1-Family life (food, religion, lifestyle), pp. 80-81

2-Music and Other Art Forms, pp. 83, 90-95

3-Language (accents, dialect, and slang), pp. 84-85

4-Holidays and Tradition, pp. 83, 89

5-Style (clothing, mannerisms, personality, etc.), pp. 86-87

Journal:

Write about some of the Africanisms that are discussed in *Black Children*.

Postscript:

Discuss some traditions and other aspects of culture that Hispanic Americans, Native Americans, and Asian Americans enjoy.

Materials:
✐ Black
    Communications
✐ Pen

Procedure:
Read and discuss
pages v-vii in *Black
Communications*

Answer these ques-
tions:
1. What is a dialect?

2. List some other
dialects that you are
familiar with.

3. Is Black English
functional in every
situation, or is it some-
times more acceptable
to use Standard En-
glish?

NOTES:

_____
_____
_____

Journal:
Write the names of
some famous African
Americans who use
Standard English. Then,
write the names of
those who use Black
English.

Listed below are five instances in which you must select the most
appropriate form of English to use. Write BE, if Black English is your
choice. Write SE, if you choose Standard English.

1. When writing a letter to a public official   _____

2. When you speak in class   _____

3. When attending a family reunion   _____

4. While being interviewed for a job   _____

5. When writing a letter to a relative   _____

Postscript:
Pretend you are an anchor person on a major network television sta-
tion and discuss some current news. For one story, use Black English,
the other, Standard English.

Materials:
- ✏ Paper
- ✏ Pen

Procedure:
Speaking in public for the first time can make you a little nervous, but it can also be very rewarding.

NOTES:
_____
_____
_____
_____
_____
_____
_____
_____
_____
_____
_____
_____
_____
_____

Journal:
Record how you felt giving a speech. Were you nervous? Do you like the way the audience responded to you?

Answer the following:

What public speakers do you enjoy listening to?

What is it about these people that captures your attention?

What styles or skills could you incorporate into your next speech?

What are some jobs that involve good public speaking skills?

Choose one of the topics listed, prepare a one to two minute speech, and present it to your class. TOPICS: "The Best Book I've Ever Read," "My Favorite Place to Visit," or "My Favorite Subject in School."

Postscript:
Ask your family, friends and classmates who their favorite speakers are and why. What do these people talk about?

Materials: (HG)
- Radio
- Music Tapes

Procedure:

Bring a tape and share it with the class. Listen to the song and try to get the message out of it.

What kind of messages do you hear played on the radio most of the time?

Are these messages positive or negative?

Do you know what kinds of music African Americans created?

NOTES:

_____

_____

_____

_____

_____

_____

Journal:

Write a song that has a positive message. It could be jazz, rap, gospel, R & B, whatever you choose. If you play a musical instrument, use it.

Your Harambee Group will be assigned one of the following categories:

   1 -- Love, and Sex

   2 -- Where to go to have fun

   3 -- Sharing and working with others

   4 -- Life

   5 -- Money

Your group should listen to the radio and write down songs that fit within your assigned category. Each group will report their findings in a class discussion.

Postscript:

Take a survey of your family and friends to find out what performers they like.

How I Spend My Time

Materials:
✏ Pen

NOTES:

_____
_____
_____
_____
_____
_____
_____
_____
_____
_____
_____
_____
_____
_____
_____
_____
_____

Procedure:
List the activities and tasks you perform regularly. Also write the length of time spent on each activity/task.

In School

1. _____
2. _____
3. _____
4. _____
5. _____

Hours/Minutes Spent

1. _____
2. _____
3. _____
4. _____
5. _____

In Your Community

1. _____
2. _____
3. _____
4. _____
5. _____

Hours/Minutes Spent

1. _____
2. _____
3. _____
4. _____
5. _____

At Home

1. _____
2. _____
3. _____
4. _____
5. _____

Hours/Minutes Spent

1. _____
2. _____
3. _____
4. _____
5. _____

Journal:
Write your responses to the following questions in the journal:
How much time do you spend working on your goal?
How could you make better use of your time?
What should you spend more time doing?

Postscript:
If you could live for 200 years, write about some of the things you would like to do.

Materials:
✏ TV
✏ Paper
✏ Pen

NOTES:

_____
_____
_____
_____
_____
_____
_____
_____
_____
_____
_____
_____
_____
_____
_____
_____
_____
_____
_____
_____
_____

Procedure:
Television shows address many different issues. Some of them include: Family, Current Events, Dating, Money, Education, Music, Nutrition, Law, History, and Politics.

Think about the shows you watch most often and decide which category each show addresses? Write the name of the show and the first letter of the appropriate category.

Television Program

1._____   2._____

3. _____   4._____

Commercials are a form of advertising. Businesses use commercials to sell their products to you, your family, your friends, and other consumers. Watch four commercials, then write the product that is being advertised.

Commercial

1._____   2._____

3. _____   4._____

Product

1._____   2._____

3. _____   4._____

Answer these questions:
1. What do you like best about television?
2. How would you improve your favorite television program?
3. Are you persuaded to buy what you see on TV?

Postscript:
Write a letter to a television producer of a show you like (or dislike) and express your opinion.

Journal:
Write about other things you like to do when you're not watching TV.

       35

Materials: (HG)
✐ *Choosing a Path*

NOTES:

_____

_____

_____

_____

_____

_____

_____

_____

_____

_____

_____

_____

_____

_____

_____

_____

_____

_____

Procedure:
Read *Choosing a Path* and discuss the message in the story. What are values? How do you obtain them? Are they important? Discuss these questions with your Harambee Group:

1. Who shows more concern for you, your family, or your friends?

2. If you had $100.00 how would you use it?

3. What is the most important thing you own?

4. How did you obtain this possession?

5. What activities do you enjoy at home or within your community?

6. What African American do you admire?

Postscript:
Discuss these questions with members of your family. Compare their responses with your own. Are they similar or different?

Journal:
Do you know anyone who has been pressured to join a gang or sell drugs? Write about ways you can help them overcome this negative form of peer pressure.

Advertising Images

Materials:
- Magazines
- Newspaper
- Abdul and the Designer Tennis Shoes

NOTES:

_____
_____
_____
_____
_____
_____
_____
_____
_____
_____
_____
_____
_____
_____
_____
_____
_____
_____

Procedure:

Cut out six advertisements and see what they are trying to sell. Is it a product, a service, or are they trying to influence your opinion about something?

What is the purpose of advertising?

What kinds of strategies are used to make you want what's being advertised or even initially grab your attention?

Even when we don't buy, are we influenced?

Advertisers generally use images that have no direct relationship to the product being advertised. For example, a beautiful woman sitting on top of a luxury car could be an advertisement for cologne.

How do these tactics influence your opinions of the product?

Journal:
Write down some of the commercials you enjoy watching and explain and why.

Postscript:
What role did advertising play in *Abdul and the Designer Tennis Shoes?*

Materials:
✎ *Abdul and the Designer Tennis Shoes*
✎ *Choosing a Path*

NOTES:
_____
_____
_____
_____
_____
_____
_____
_____
_____
_____
_____
_____
_____
_____
_____
_____
_____
_____
_____

Procedure:
Examine the lives of the two major characters in *Abdul and the Designer Tennis Shoes* and *Choosing a Path*. Their experiences at school were quite different. Write down some of the things they did at school and what school must have meant to each of them, the boy who sold drugs in school and the boy who played basketball.

Consider the following:

How can education affect your future career choices?

How can education expose you to new ideas and information?

Journal:
Write about the significance of education in helping you to achieve your goals.

Postscript:
Education is not a process that ends with school but continues throughout one's life. Interview entrepreneurs in your community to find the role education played in helping them achieve their business goals.

Materials:
✏ Paper
✏ Markers

Procedure:
Consider the following:

Friends can play a significant role in how we develop.

Do your friends help you to become a better person?

Do your friends encourage you to get into trouble?

Do you need friends that help you get into trouble? Why?

NOTES:

_____
_____
_____
_____
_____
_____
_____

Friendship

Complete the following questions by providing information about your best friend.

1. My best friend is _____.
2. We have been good friends for _____ years.
3. We like to _____ together.
4. After school, we often _____.
5. My best friend helps me _____.
6. What I like most about my friend is _____.

Journal:
Record some of the nice things you and your favorite friend have done together.

Postscript:
Make a drawing of your friends or the kind of people that you would like to have as friends. Role play about a good friend that is helpful and tries to do something to keep you out of trouble.

Materials:
✎ *Shining Legacy*

NOTES:

_____

_____

_____

_____

_____

_____

_____

_____

_____

_____

_____

_____

_____

_____

_____

_____

_____

_____

Procedure:

In the African court and in other societies, there is a court of judges typically called a Council of Elders. They would act as advisers for anyone needing their assistance. Many people enjoyed the benefits of the Council's wisdom and experience.

You have your own Council of Elders. They consist of your parents, teacher, pastor, and other members of your extended family. Be sure to ask for help when you need to.

Why is it important to be able to think for yourself?

Should you follow the crowd?

When a crowd is doing something dangerous or life threatening, how can you avoid pressure to participate?

Journal:

Write down an instance when someone tried to get you to do something you knew was wrong and you had the courage to stand up to them.

Postscript:

Look through *Shining Legacy* and find two people whose lives exemplify strength of character and the ability to say no to things that they felt were wrong. Discuss these people.

Materials: (HG)
✐ Coloring Materials
✐ Shining Legacy,
    p. 40-47

Procedure:
Nguzo Saba is Kiswahili for seven principles. The Nguzo Saba consists of qualities that make our lives and our communities better. Read pages 40-47 in *Shining Legacy*.

Nguzo Saba
African Value System
Umoja (Unity)
Kujichagulia
    (Self-determination)
Ujima (Collective Work
    and Responsibility)
Ujamaa (Cooperative
    Economics)
Nia (Purpose)
Kuumba (Creativity)
Imani (Faith)

Discuss each principle and how you can use it in everyday life. Decorate your classroom with African art, the liberation flag and the seven candles of Kwanzaa
(3 red, 1 black, 3 green).

Journal:
Record your impressions of Kwanzaa. Has your family ever celebrated Kwanzaa?

Postscript:
With your encouragement, maybe your teacher can set aside a day when students can bring a variety of African foods, i.e.: avocado, plantain, watermelon, millet, okra, blackeyed peas, yams, seafood and chicken curry.

Materials:
✏ Your Creative Minds

NOTES:
_____
_____
_____
_____
_____
_____
_____
_____
_____
_____
_____
_____
_____
_____
_____
_____
_____
_____
_____

Journal:
Write down how you like to creatively express yourself. Is it in writing, drawing, dancing, singing, etc.?

Kuumba Means Creativity

Procedure:
Kuumba is the 6th principle of the Nguzo Saba (seven principles). It means Creativity - to always do as much as you can, in the way that you can in order to leave your community more beautiful and beneficial than when you inherited it. Think of something you could do to make your neighborhood more beautiful.

Consider the following:

Why is our community dirty in some areas?

Who litters in our community?

How can we use Kuumba for our community?

For our homes?

Postscript:
Discuss what creativity means. Then name some of the things that we can do creatively today that could not have been done 200 years ago.

Materials:
🖉 *Motivating Black Youth, p 34-44*

Procedure:
Read pages 34-44 in *Motivating*, then answer these questions:

1. What talents do you have that could be used in your own business?

2. What type of business would you like to start someday?

3. How could classmates, family, or friends help you?

Create a student business club in your school. Use organizations such as cheerleaders, student council, athletic teams, or clubs. What "products" could be made and sold?

Journal:
Record your impressions about some of the most successful people in America. What type of businesses do they have? How many of them practice Ujamaa?
Are any of them African American?

Ujamaa - Cooperative Economics

Postscript:
Do you have an organization in your school or neighborhood where you can learn the principles of business and economics. If not, why not? Who can help you put a small junior business club together?

Materials:
✏ *To Be Popular or Smart*, p. 1-10

Listed below are some qualities and behavior that apply to men and women. In front of each item, write the name of the group that is appropriate.

Write Men, Women, or Both.

_____Make babies

_____Wash dishes

_____Cry

_____Hurt someone

_____Budget money

_____Study

_____Be responsible

_____Curse often

_____Have babies

Journal:
Write a letter to someone that you admire. Explain why you admire him or her and identify the qualities you would like to emulate.

Becoming a Man or Woman

Procedure:
Read the chapter on Student Profiles (pages 1-10) in *To Be Popular or Smart*, then write the name of the character next to the quality he/she demonstrates.

_____ Responsible

_____ Wears fancy designer clothes

_____ Maintains good grades

_____ Has several boyfriends or girlfriends

Postscript:
Using the qualities previously mentioned, write questions to ask men and women in your school, home and community. What are their definitions of manhood and womanhood? Are they similar to yours?

The SETCLAE Student Profile

Instructions

Please answer the following questions on the answer sheet and think very hard about how you feel before answering each one. THERE ARE NO RIGHT OR WRONG ANSWERS. WE WANT YOUR ANSWERS.

Part I

Read each statement or question. If it is true for you, circle the letter "a". If it is not true for you, circle "b". Answer every question, even if it's hard to decide. (Just think about yourself and what's important to you.) Select only one answer for each question.

1. I like to be alone sometimes.   a. Yes   b. No

2. I enjoy public speaking.   a. Yes   b. No

3. Cleaning up should be done collectively.   a. Yes   b. No

4. School will help me to accomplish my own goals.   a. Yes   b. No

5. I enjoy looking for positive things to say about people.   a. Yes   b. No

6. I have personal goals.   a. Yes   b. No

7. I would rather do an extra credit project
   by myself than with a small group.   a. Yes   b. No

8. I get upset when things don't go my way.   a. Yes   b. No

9. School is boring most of the time.   a. Yes   b. No

10. I speak more than one dialect.   a. Yes   b. No

11. If I don't see a trash can, I throw my trash on the ground. a. Yes   b. No

12. I like participating in special projects
    like science fairs and spelling bees.   a. Yes   b. No

13. When the truth is hard to say, I don't say it.   a. Yes   b. No

14. My friends are more important to me than my family.   a. Yes   b. No

15. My neighborhood is a good place to live in.   a. Yes   b. No

16. I can get any job I want, if I work at it hard enough.　　a. Yes　　b. No

17. I like being with people that are different from me.　　a. Yes　　b. No

18. I like me!　　a. Yes　　b. No

19. Do you believe you can have your own
business when you get older?　　a. Yes　　b. No

20. The contribution I make to the world is not as
important as the contributions of more famous people.　　a. Yes　　b. No

21. African Americans have not made many achievements
in math, science, technology, and business.　　a. Yes　　b. No

22. If I could, I would make friends with people of all races.　　a. Yes　　b. No

23. Black people are not able to compete with
others in many areas.　　a. Yes　　b. No

24. I want to be able to speak Standard
English in certain situations.　　a. Yes　　b. No

Part II

Read each item carefully. If it is something that is important to you, select "a". If it is not important to you (it doesn't really matter or has nothing to do with you), select "b". Take your time and think about it. THERE ARE NO RIGHT OR WRONG ANSWERS. WE WANT TO KNOW YOUR FEELINGS.

1. Helping others　　a. Important to me　　b. Not important to me

2. What others think of me　　a. Important to me　　b. Not important to me

3. Reading in a study group　　a. Important to me　　b. Not important to me

4. Television as a way to receive
most of my information　　a. Important to me　　b. Not important to me

5. Solving problems by fighting　　a. Important to me　　b. Not important to me

6. Learning about my family
members - dead and living　　a. Important to me　　b. Not important to me

7. Working with others on short and
long-term projects　　a. Important to me　　b. Not important to me

8. Doing whatever my friends do   a. Important to me   b. Not important to me

9. Wearing expensive clothes   a. Important to me   b. Not important to me

10. Doing well in school   a. Important to me   b. Not important to me

11. Speaking up for myself and
    my ideas   a. Important to me   b. Not important to me

12. Being positive most of the time   a. Important to me   b. Not important to me

13. Living conditions in Africa   a. Important to me   b. Not important to me

Part III

Read each statement carefully. Read the choices and select "a" if the statement accurately describes you and your feelings. Select "b" if the statement does not accurately describe you and your feelings.
If asked to describe my personality to someone I'd never met, I would use statements like:

1. a leader   a. Yes   b. No

2. confident   a. Yes   b. No

3. mature   a. Yes   b. No

4. critical of others   a. Yes   b. No

5. proud of my culture   a. Yes   b. No

6. easily bored   a. Yes   b. No

7. Africa is a dark continent filled with hunger,
   poverty and ignorance.   a. True   b. False

8. I can list five living African American men that are doing positive things in their family, business, church, community, or some other organization.
   List them below.

1) _____

2) _____

3) _____

4) _____

5) _____

9. Select the one that is most important to you. Choose only one!
   a. being popular   b. doing well in school

Part IV

Read the following statements and choices for answers carefully. Then pick the answer that most accurately describes your feelings. Circle the letter in front of your answer.

THERE ARE NO RIGHT OR WRONG ANSWERS. Choose the answer that is right for YOU.

1. When my friends have fun without me, I
   a. am happy that they are having fun.
   b. don't even think about it.
   c. wish they weren't having fun without me.

2. When I hear something negative about a person, I
   a. can't wait to tell someone else.
   b. talk to the person to see how I can help.
   c. try to find out more, because it's interesting.

3. When someone says something about me that is not good but is true, I
   a. get upset.
   b. don't want to be around them anymore.
   c. listen and learn from their observations.

4. When someone makes fun of me,
   a. I get upset.
   b. I am hurt.
   c. I laugh with them.
   d. I make a joke of it.
   e. I don't like it.

5. When I am talking to someone, most of the time I look
   a. at their hands.
   d. into their eyes.
   c. at the floor.
   d. all around.

6. I always make sure I am neat and clean in my appearance:
   a. never
   b. once in a while
   c. most of the time

7. Money is important for:
   a. buying expensive clothes
   b. building the community in which we live
   c. buying whatever I want
   d. saving for future plans

8. A girl becomes a woman when (select the answer that is most important to you),
   a. she has a baby.
   b. her body becomes more developed (she has breasts and hair under her arms).
   c. she takes care of herself and her family.
   d. she can talk back to her mother.
   e. she has a boyfriend.

48

9. When I do poorly on my schoolwork, I
   a. don't really care.
   b. know I tried my best.
   c. know I should try harder.
   d. know it's only because I can't do any better.
   e. know the teacher gave us work that was too hard or boring.

10. In my involvement with organizations, I
    a. like to hold a leadership position.
    b. like to work as a team.
    c. don't like doing the dirty work.
    d. often disagree with other members.

11. When I need help, I
    a. get frustrated.
    b. ask for it.
    c. try to figure it out myself.

12. I pick my friends because
    a. they look good.
    b. they are cool.
    c. they are understanding.
    d. they have something to offer me.

13. I am glad I am the race I am.
    a. Yes   b. No

14. I chose the answer above because
    a. I am proud of my heritage.
    b. I should be glad.
    c. I study my history and culture.
    d. my friends say it's important.

15. I like my favorite music because
    a. of its rhythm for dancing.
    b. of its positive messages.
    c. of its ability to help me relax.
    d. the rappers curse and insult women.
    e. the videos are nice.

16. A boy becomes a man when
    a. he can handle drugs and crime.
    b. he makes a baby.
    c. he takes responsibility for his actions.
    d. he can fight well.

17. When I attend assemblies or special events, I like to sit
    a. in the middle of the auditorium.
    b. in the front of the auditorium.
    c. in the back of the auditorium.

18. When I set a goal, I
    a. expect someone to make it happen for me.
    b. plan how I will do it and make the first step.
    c. just think about it very hard.
    d. ask my friends to get me started.

19. When the teacher leaves the room, I
    a. talk.
    b. stop doing my work.
    c. look at who is being disobedient.
    d. find something quiet to do once I finish my work.

20. Learning about one's culture and heritage is very important and helps me feel good about who I am.
    a. Yes
    b. No

21. I like my favorite television program because
    a. it's very funny.
    b. I enjoy the action.
    c. I enjoy the "scenery" (cars, clothes, houses, etc.).
    d. it is educational.
    e. it makes me think and discuss important issues with others.

22. I am beautiful because I have
    a. light skin.
    b. dark skin.
    c. natural hair.
    d. long hair.
    e. a thin shape.

23. Answering these questions was
    a. very enjoyable.
    b. no big deal.
    c. a good way to take a closer look at my personal development.

24. Africa has many cities.
    a. True   b. False

25. Africa is the Motherland of Black people all over the world.
    a. True   b. False

26. Egypt, also known as Kemet (which means Land of the Blacks) is in Africa, which is the cradle of civilization.
    a. True   b. False

27. African people have always resisted domination all over the world.
    a. True   b. False

28. Africa is mostly jungle.
    a. True   b. False

29. Tarzan movies show you what Africa is like and used to be like.
    a. True   b. False

30. Africa is a continent on which there is a cultural unity more important than the differences we hear about in the news.
    a. True   b. False

Using the definitions on the right, place the letter that you feel best describes each of the seven principles listed (Nguzo Saba).

____ 31. UMOJA

a. to build our stores and businesses and profit from them together

____ 32. KUJICHAGULIA

b. to have a collective goal of building and developing our community

____ 33. UJIMA

c. to always be creative in the ways we improve our communities

____ 34. UJAMAA

d. being determined to speak up for ourselves

____ 35. NIA

e. to work on challenges together and feel responsible as a group

____ 36. KUUMBA

f. to believe in ourselves that we will do great things

____ 37. IMANI

g. to keep in touch with and offer support to friends, neighbors, and community

SOMETHING YOU SHOULD KNOW

Group # 2 - African Countries
Nigeria --------This West African country is Africa's most populated country. It is rich with oil.

Kenya ---------This beautiful East African country is home for the Gikuyu community. Jomo Kenyatta led them to freedom.

Egypt ----------Civilization began here. It is home of the great pyramids, temples, tombs and King Tut.

Azania---------Sometimes called South Africa, it is a country filled with gold and diamonds. We all must remove apartheid, a form of slavery. Azania is the home of Nelson Mandela.

Tanzania -----It is an East African country and home of the great former President Julius Nyerere.

Group # 3 - African Communities
Ashanti -------A community from Ghana. Many residents work as weavers of beautiful kente cloth and carvers of the Ashanti stool for the king.

Chagga -------A community where the children play among others the same age and are taught to be adults by the time they are 15 years old.

Pondo ---------A community where the children learn self-defense at an early age.

Fanti -----------A community in West Africa. They pour libation which is pouring a little wine on the ground to honor their dead family members (ancestors)

Ikoma ----------A community in West Africa. They gather honey to eat and sell.

Group # 4 - Black Colleges
Morehouse
College -------An all-male school in Atlanta, Georgia. Martin Luther King, Jr. and Spike Lee graduated from Morehouse.

Hampton
University ----A college in Hampton, Virginia with 4500 students. They have their own radio and TV stations.

Spelman
College -------An all-female school with nearly 200 students. It's right next door to Morehouse College. Bill and Camille Cosby gave the school $20 million dollars in 1988.

Tuskegee
Institute -------Founded by Booker T. Washington. They have a pre-veterinarian program (animal doctors). It's in Tuskegee, Alabama.

Howard
University ----One of the largest Black colleges in the country. It's in

SETCLAE PRONUNCIATION GLOSSARY

Kiswahili

Phonics
- a-short a
- e-long a
- u-long u
- i-long e
- o-long o

Jambo - Hello	Njema - Fine
Habari Gani - What is the news?	Asante - Thank you
Asante Sana - Thank you very much	Mama - Mother
Baba - Father	Ndada - Sister
Ndugu - Brother	Watoto - Children
Mtoto - Child	Mwalimu - Teacher
Mwanafunzi - Student	Shule - School
Yebo - Yes	La - No
Acha - Stop	Ujima - Collective work & responsibility
Ujamaa - Cooperative economics	Harambee - Let's pull together
Pamoja Tutashinda - Together we will win	Mzee - Elder
Chakula - Food	Choo - Toilet
Hodi hodi - Hurry	Tutaonana - Goodbye
Moja - One	Mbili - Two
Tatu - Three	Nne - Four
Tano - Five	Sita - Six
Saba - Seven	Nane - Eight
Tisa - Nine	Kumi - Ten
Umoja - Unity	Nisamehe - Excuse me
Tafadali - Please	Mzuri - Good
Mia - Purpose	Imani - Faith
Kuumba - Creativity	